Understanding the Command of God for a Chosen People

By Kim Y. Jackson

Nikki,

God Bless You.

Worship in Spirit
& in Truth.

Minister Kim Jackson

TRUE WORSHIP

Published and Cover Design by
God's Glory Publishing

*"True Worship - Understanding the Command of God
for a Chosen People"*

by Kim Y. Jackson

Copyright© 2006

ISBN 10: 0-9743749-1-1

ISBN 13: 978-0-9743749-1-8

Scripture quotations are taken from the (NKJV) New King James Version and (NIV) New International Version of the Bible.

TRUE WORSHIP

God's Glory Publishing

<u>*Acknowledgments*</u>

To God be the Glory, Great things He has done.

God there is none that can compare to you. Thank you for allowing me to experience you in Worship. I am awestruck at your love, grace and power. Every encounter that I have with you leaves me in awe. You have captivated me and leave me desiring more of you. Again and again you have shown me that "the things that seem impossible with man are possible with God." You've shown me if I would just enter in, seek your face, surrender and worship you that you will handle everything. Hallelujah. I love you Lord!

*"But the hour cometh,
and now is when the true
worshippers shall
worship the Father in
Spirit and in Truth:
for the Father seeketh
such to worship Him"
(John 4:23)*

Table of Contents

Introduction

God has made a call for true worshippers but the question remains, have the elect of God answered the call? The Bible reveals a direct command to the church from God in John 4:23 that states, ***"But the hour cometh, and now is when the true worshippers shall worship the Father in Spirit and in truth: for the Father seeketh such to worship him."*** However, the question still remains have we said yes to His command. For all Christians who have been redeemed by Jesus Christ as he hung lifeless on the cross, worship is a requirement -- not an option. Why is it that the call for true worship has not been answered? Could the reason why the church of the only True and Living God not obey the command to worship lie in the fact that we do not know: who we are called to worship, what is a worshipper, why we worship, how to worship, where we are to worship, when we are to worship, what is the order of worship or even what are the benefits of worship? The answers to these questions are unveiled in the life of believers who are sincere and desire to enter into full relationship with God [and through the biblically instructed, anointed teaching of God's word about Worship.

Through my life experience and research, I have identified there is a "Plight of Christianity for True Worship" evidenced in the lack of knowledge of the believer, of God's command for worship, lack of intimacy with God through worship and the lack of Biblical instruction regarding worship.

The word "Plight" is used to identify and define a spiritual condition needing a spiritual solution. Once the solution to this spiritual condition is found and implemented, a change is manifested in the life of the believer. As a result, the believer is transformed. Within the pages of this book are written testimonies of several worship leaders who reveal their personal revelation concerning God and worship. A personal account of their love for God is written herein substantiating the need of God's elect to answer the call to worship, why they worship and openly disclose the relationship they have with God as a result of intimate worship.

While preparing my thesis entitled "The Plight of Christianity for True Worship" I used a 25 - question survey administered to 100 respondents to ascertain their knowledge, belief and understanding of worship. I found that most of the responses to the survey were found to be on an intermediate level. However, the saints of God need to go deeper in our relationship with God and experience "True Worship." Within the contents of this book "True Worship-Understanding the command of God for a chosen people," you will find Biblical Instructions on Worship, along with personal reflections from God's elect true worshippers to provide evidence of the need of the believer in Christ to exercise True Worship unto God. True Worship is required because it directly affects our relationship with God. Research compiled from the thesis entitled "The Plight of Christianity for True Worship" provided specific answers to questions from the survey, biblically directed teaching on true worship and personal reflections noted by some of God's elect worshippers substantiating the need of today's church to follow the command of God to worship Him in Spirit and in Truth.

"True Worship - Understanding the command of God for a chosen people" answers questions about worship. This instructional tool can be used as a manual to provide the people of God with a greater understanding of the command of God for "True Worship" as is written in John 4:23.

"True Worship"

Chapter 1:

"But the Hour Cometh and Now Is"

Chapter 1: "But the Hour Cometh and Now Is"

I.   God's call for Worship

A. His Command

God's word declares in John 4:23 ***"But the hour cometh, and now is when the true worshippers shall worship the Father in Spirit and in Truth: for the Father seeketh such to worship Him."*** The Apostle John wrote these words in approximately 85 A.D. about Jesus speaking to the woman at the well in Samaria. This scripture from John 4:23 not only changed the life of the woman at the well but also brought clarity to the life of every believer concerning worshipping God. Through this scripture God sent forth His command that would change the intent of the relationship of the believer in Christ and the Lord God.

A specific state of time was called forth from heaven for the very elect of God to receive direction on how believers are to express our admiration and celebrate God. The King of Kings commanded this direction for the believers who were not just verbally truthful, but to those who were sincere and had character that exuded integrity. One might ask, "Why did God elicit His son Jesus to speak these words"? The answer is that God desired and searched for believers such as these. He knew that the true worshippers would be drawn to fulfill this mandate without hesitation. We serve a God of all power who created us to worship only. He wanted us His creation to seek after His heart, express freely how we feel about Him and to celebrate Him. God wanted this expression to be pure, free, uninhibited and uninfluenced by anyone or anything.

God sought after a few whom He would call a "True Worshipper". These people were those who would sacrifice their own personal concerns even in the midst of chaos and worship Him. These chosen (few with the title "True Worshipper") would follow after God's biblical direction and experience Him in all of His goodness.

B. *Our Relationship with God*

Our relationship with God motivates us to follow God's command to worship Him. As we seek a closer relationship with God, we begin to experience His power and He reveals His majesty. True Worshippers seek for more than a one-time experience with God. They find that eternal secret place of privilege before the Almighty King that releases them into a place of joy, peace and blessings forever. They find out that God's word is true that says, "in thy presence is fullness of joy, at thy right hand there are pleasures forever more", Psalm 16:11. True Worshippers seek after and receive an intimate relationship with God. This experience is attributed to the affection and love personified in their expressed celebration and value of God and of His abilities. As "True Worshippers", we come into a place of new fellowship "with God." We express the value associated with our relationship through the act of worship. Luke 7:37-38 speaks of the value of the woman who wiped Jesus' feet had for her Master and Lord. She poured fine perfume on His feet and wiped them with her hair. Notice that the perfume had an exorbitant value for that time period. But the devotion that the woman felt towards Jesus prompted her to give Him something of great value, to express her genuine feelings and value for Him. She valued Jesus more than anything. Her act of worship was indicative of her love for him, beyond any personal possession.

This woman's act of anointing Jesus' feet released an eternal value. The fragrance of the perfume was temporary. However, just like the woman, Jesus associated a value with her act of worship, which was far greater than her possession of oil. He knew that she was worshipping Him because of their relationship. When we worship, there is to be a clear motive of appreciation and celebration relative to our relationship with God. Isn't it clear that we are to lie at His feet to worship Him? Aren't we supposed to into the presence of God at home, in our churches and sanctuaries with a purpose to lie before the feet of Jesus to worship Him?

Mary served Jesus through her act of worship. She took on a servant's heart to bless Him. When we become servants, we are saying "Jesus, trust me to bless others who you call your own. If the Body of Chris cannot lay at the feet of Jesus and worship Him, how can we possibly think that He will entrust us to minister to His people? This principle is relational.

Our relationship with God is everything. To have a relationship means that we are able to relate, communicate, and be touch each other. Every time we pray, we are seeking a closer relationship with Jesus. Prayer is not a one-sided conversation, it is two-sided. It is a means by which we engage with the Most High God. Through this encounter He tells us those "great and unsearchable things you do not know", Jeremiah 33:3. What does prayer have to do with relationship and worship? Everything! Through prayer, we grow closer to God and receive the revelation of who God is. Worship makes our relationship personal and enables us to celebrate Him freely. Prayer cannot be conducted without worship. If we do not have this relationship, He won't give His precious revelation to those who won't engage in a conversation with Him in prayer.

When we value our relationship with God we don't take it for granted. Worship becomes a daily opportunity to speak and relate to the "Author and Finisher of our Faith", Hebrews 12:2. We are to rise daily to seek an encounter with the "Master." By daily seeking God's face through worship, we show God that He is important. The word of God clearly tells us that we are to "Seek ye first the Kingdom of God and His Righteousness and all these things will be added unto you as well, Matthew 6:33. When we seek Him first, there are benefits that are released and we receive them through the demonstration of our Worship of Him. God manifests His power to destroy yolks and lift burdens through worship. Without worshipping Him, God is not compelled to bless, heal or even manifest His power sovereignly. As a Christian growing daily through the word of God, we are to never feel that we should miss the opportunity to worship God. I admonish every believer in Christ to "worship unto God" every day. This daily act of submission is necessary so that "when we step onto a platform and break open that vessel, only the pure, holy and undefiled oil of worship will flow out".[1]

God doesn't want a relationship as a prerequisite to Worship, He requires it. Believers cannot possibly speak of His grace and mercy if we don't have a relationship by which we can attest to who He is and what He has done for us. It is quite stunning to find that many in the house of God are not taking worship seriously. There are some people in congregations who purposely don't come to church during worship. Could the reason be that the

---

[1] Pastor Rod Parsley with Clint Brown, <u>Praise, the Ultimate Experience - Worship, the Ultimate Relationship,</u>
(Columbus, Ohio: Results Publishing, 1992) 79.

importance of worship is not taught thoroughly?

19

Chapter 2:

"When the True Worshippers Shall Worship the Father"

Chapter 2: When the True Worshippers Shall Worship the Father

I.   The Plight of Christianity for True Worship

A. The Case for Worship

Through personal experience, I have seen many members of the body of Christ either ignore or not accept the command of Worship. It is only through the leading of the Holy Spirit in Worship that the saints of God are able to commune with our God who is Holy and righteous. The Bible declares in John 4:23 (NIV), ***"But the hour cometh, and now is when the True Worshippers shall Worship the Father in Spirit and in Truth: for the Father seeketh such to Worship Him.*** When Jesus spoke these words, it was a didactic command to last throughout eternity. He exercised the gift that God had given Him to inform God's chosen people "that the time had come for those persons chosen by God, with a character exuding integrity, lead by His Father's spirit, to come boldly to the throne of grace to express and celebrate the divine nature of God." Because this word in John 4:23 is spoken as a command, it is evident that God saw a need to remind the saints of God of why we were created, and that was to worship Him. To God, it was important that this part of our relationship no longer be ignored or denied. That is why; He made it a command without an option. God took the time to explain the timing of the spirit realm. The time was at hand to follow-through on the task by which the believer was called to perform a life-changing act. He took the time to state the character of the people who were called to perform this act.

21

Lastly, He expressed in this scripture that He sought a people who would sacrifice everything to perform this divine act and to hold the title of True Worshippers. The significance of this command was that God knew that the people He had created to Worship Him would choose to exercise free will in worship. Unfortunately, there are some that chose to worship idols instead of worshipping the only True and Living God. Acts of worship not geared toward God is idolatry. By committing idolatry they have slowed down the progression of the work of God individually and corporately. The church today must take a stand to Worship God as His command directs us to. When God comes He is looking for a church without discord and strife. He is looking for a church on one accord. It is of the utmost importance that the church of God comes together to follow this command of worship.

For as much as we serve a God who is the same yester-day, today and forever more, God is calling for a new order of worship in the church. That order is to put aside the old stereotypical manner by which we worship Him. He wants the believer to be free in worship and to also acknowledge the manifestation of His spirit in Worship. Before God breathed life into man, He knew that we would revert to ways of worship (idolatry and other repetitive religious acts) that would not honor Him. Therefore, He knew we would need a word of correction and direction that He established and commanded in John 4:23 (NIV) declaring, ***"But the hour cometh, and now is when the true worshippers shall worship the Father in Spirit and in truth: for the Father seeketh such to worship Him."*** Even though this word was spoken once, it will forever be heard throughout eternity. Christianity must come to the recurrent knowledge by which we were created and that is to worship God. God knows the true nature of man. So He established a mechanism by which He could speak to the generations to remind us to come back to the predestined call of man, to Worship Him in Spirit and in Truth. We have read and understood this command, so why don't we worship Him? Is it that our carnal nature still will not yield to our Spirit man? To worship God encompasses opening our mouths to make an expressed description of the value that we have for God. As a result of our intimate personal relationship with Him we should have an infinite selection of words by which we worship God. Through these words of expression, the Holy Spirit takes over and begins to direct us in the Spirit on worshipping the *(El-Shadai)* the Almighty God. But why don't we take the time to express our sincere gratitude that He is our Savior. Certainly, thanks and gratitude are where we are to start. Through our Salvation Jesus performed a miracle. So why don't we express our acknowledgement that He is our Savior, Lord, Sovereign King, Miracle Worker, King of Kings, Lord of Lords, Rock, Provider, Healer, Author and Finisher of our Faith, Advocate, Redeemer, Bread of life, Living Water, Good Shepherd, Anchor, Prince of Peace, Mighty God and so much more? There is so much to be said to celebrate and express our value of God. Although Worship is a key element in our relationship with God, it is often either passively taught or not whole-heartedly accepted as a command for the all of God's people. Worship should be a passion on the hearts of all believers and not just a second thought. When the Body of Christ takes hold of this passion for Worship a work is performed in the heavenlies. Strangely enough, after 2000 years, we have regressed in our expressed Worship towards God and have not yet begun to tap into the manifestation in the heavenlics that is associated with Worship. God had a perfectly designed pattern of worship, and that order of worship is written of in His word. The pattern of True Worship is implemented through participation.

B. *Religious Acts of Repetition*

One question that often surfaces is "Why Has Worship become a religious act without purpose to the body of Christ." To this end many churches have enabled a tradition that has no impact upon God, much less upon any realm of the spirit. Why has the church taken this position? Could it be that some members are turned off by other members in the congregation who freely worship? Specifically, I am talking about the ones that demonstrate their oneness with God on a level in which many are not accustomed to or familiar with? These demonstrations may include Christians who bow or lay prostrate in the house of God. Some lift their hands, while others sing songs and play instruments. Others speak words of edification to the Body of Christ, while some others dance. These are some forms of Worship that can only be done through the leading of the Holy Spirit. When God's people seek His face, these demonstrations of worship are no longer perceived as a ritual or an act. They are in fact the modes by which God uses the believer to minister in the congregation among other believers to God Himself. It is the way by which God chooses to anoint men and women on an individual basis, to touch His heart and to express their worship (worthship) towards Him.

C. *Passive Approach to Worship*

The church as it stands today has become passive in its approach to worship. We should not be passive. Worshipping passively means that we consider our relationship with the only True and Living God as menial. In worship, we are to actively participate. It is here that we meet God. The bible says "therefore come bodly unto the throne of grace, that we may obtain mercy, and find grace to help in the time of need", (Hebrews 4:16) and to "enter into His Gates with thanksgiving and into His courts with praise; be thankful unto Him and bless His name", (Psalms 100:4). The opposite of passive is active. When we take an active approach towards worship we are anxiously awaiting opportunities to enter into the presence of the Almighty God to worship Him. It is then that we leave ourselves free and open unto minister to God.

D. *Free Expression in Worship*

Christians should be free to celebrate God in our very own distinctive personal ways. It should not be an offense that a brother or sister in Christ moves with the Spirit of God in worship. A question should spark in the minds of the blood washed believer of Christ when they don't see other Christians who don't worship and when they don't exercise an open means of communicating, celebrating and declaring the goodness of God in their lives. Worship should not be a struggle. When we release ourselves to submit to the will of God in worship, the Spirit of God begins to manifest our declaration of God's magnificence in our lives. As a result we are free to experience God in all of His fullness. The scriptures declare "Now the Lord is that Spirit, and where the Spirit of the Lord is, there is liberty", (2 Corinthians 3:17). This liberty begins to show in every area of our lives as we continuously submit to our homes, workplaces, family, personal relationships, finances, and personal worship to God in worship. Even the opportunities that Christians have to minister and share the word of God should be submitted to Him during worship. There is exponential freedom taking place when we continuously submit to God through worship that often times cannot be explained. The more we worship, the more we are changed into the same image from Glory to Glory, even as by the Spirit of the Lord," (2 Corinthians 3:18).

E. *Interruption of Benefits*

As an active participant of "True Worship" of God, there is a release of benefits from the heavenlies. When we choose not to participate in worship and/or we ignore the command to worship, we are saying to God that we are not interested in the blessings that He has set aside for us. To say we are not interested in worship sets the stage for divine intervention to become interrupted. A supernatural outpouring from heavens windows becomes suspended. This is not the course that the saints of God should follow. We must honor God's command. A willful act of disobedience against worship can cause death to our spirit man and seed. The word of God admonishes us with the following statement "Now choose life, so that <u>you and your children may live</u>", Deuteronomy 30:19. The acts of Worship are acknowledged by God, and they have perpetual benefits.

F. *Lost Emphasis on Teaching on Worship*

Interestingly enough, a topic that has yet to be thoroughly evaluated is teaching on worship. Could the reason why so many of the saints of God do not worship God in "Spirit and in Truth" be because they have no idea of what worshipping the Most High God is all about? This lack of knowledge includes the purpose of worship and it's various forms. Yes, the Holy Spirit "reveals all truths and teaches all things." However; the saints of God have a responsibility to teach the word of God concerning all biblical truths to each other. A major emphasis for the body of Christ is to teach the Gospel of Jesus Christ. Furthermore, teaching is one of the five-fold ministries of the Gospel of Jesus Christ. So we ought not to neglect teaching on worship, which is a key component to our relationship with God. When we teach the full word of God, Christians will begin to comprehend the concept stated in Colossians 1:10, "growing in the knowledge of God". Teachers have the ultimate responsibility to teach the unadulterated word of God, even for Worship. He would not have us to be ignorant." With it, comes a greater reward for all of the saints of God.

G. *Personal plight*

For over 25 years, I attended one church and to this day I cannot recall one teaching on "Worship." At the age of twelve, I gave my life to Christ. I had been attending the same church since I was seven. In my mind, I believed that there was supposed to be a significant change in my life because I said yes to Jesus and walked down the long aisle of the church. We sang songs; yet, I never saw or experienced a manifestation of the Holy Spirit moving in my life. I participated in the women's ministry like the rest of the women in the church, sang on the choir like other people who could sing, I even lead a youth group when I was pregnant with my second child. On Sunday, we had church as usual. Then, one day my son's God father said "I know of a church that is closer to where you live and I would like for you to meet me there." When I entered the doors of the church, I met the True and Living God, the real Jesus, along with the Holy Spirit. My life as it was would never be the same. Under the tutelage of Pastor Mark Saunders, I was exposed to the unadulterated word of God, which included teaching on worship and the anointing of God. Under the tutelage of this man of God, I found the only True and Living God, and began to "Worship Him in Spirit and in Truth." Blessed be the Name of the Lord.

My exposure to, teachings and understanding of Worship did not stop there. Several years later, I was lead to the Life Builders Church, formally known as Zion Temple Fellowship Church. At Life Builders Church under the Pastorate of Bishop J. Charles Carrington, Jr., the ministering spirit of God revealed truths concerning worship in an even deeper dimension. I was taken from the outer courts of the temple, through the inner court, and into the Holy of Holies.

From my worship experiences under Bishop J. Charles Carrington, Jr. along with Pastor Mark Saunders, I have came to know God in a more intimate way. My passion and love for God is expressed in various forms during Worship. In addition, I am able to see and experience the anointing that rests upon the men and women who lead God's people into worship. Through the anointing of God, I found a sweet rest and relief from the ever-present forces that come against me, when I enter into the presence of God and pursue God through True Worship.

H. *The Position of Today's Church in Worship*

The more I experience God in Worship, the more I want my brothers and sisters in Christ to experience God, but in a different dimension from what they are accustomed. It often grieves me when I come into a church and the position of the church is lackadaisical when it comes to worship. A key element to the maintenance of our relationship with God is, worship and it should be taught and emphasized continuously, just like the Gospels. If the church does not follow the command of John 4:23, then believers are doomed to live a life separated from God. We will forever go through the motions in a worship service, never touch the heart of God, nor make an impact upon the Kingdom of God or the forces of darkness.

Within today's church, the biggest hindrances to growth in worship are education of the saints of God and our submission to the leading of the Holy Spirit. When we educate the body, we are more equipped with knowledge to understand the work and purpose of worship, and to lead others in worship. Likewise, when we submit ourselves to the Spirit of God, we release the control of our lives into the hands of God. To do either or both of these things requires a heart and a desire for God's presence to perform a supernatural work through and in our lives. It is quite evident that the work of God is perfect and when we release all control into his hands, our lives are complete, healthy and whole. "For the joy of the Lord is our strength", Nehemiah 8:10. Once this principle is fully realized among God's people, the Gospel will spread faster and so much further.

Today's church needs to step back and exam its position in worship today. Examine individual motives in worship as well as any self-imposed inhibitions. If we have a desire to be in church because it is a rule that we grew up with, then our motives are wrong. However, if our motives are true and genuine and we are coming to seek the face of God, we will experience Him in True Worship.

Man though created by God, is unfortunately ritualistic. We do things because we are used to doing them and not out of a response of our love for God. Today's church must recognize that we cannot do things as we did before. We serve a progressive God, so we cannot possibly participate in worship in the same manner. God is progressive and He requires us to take a progressive step in worship. It's not enough to sing from a hymn book. He is calling today's church to sing from the heart. God wants to manifest Himself through His spirit. He wants to change the traditional forms of worship and release us to experience Him in a supernatural way. God's way of worship can only be done through our submission to Him and then, we can experience His fullness in "True Worship."

II.   Research

A. Methods

In order to substantiate my hypothesis for "The Plight of Christianity for True Worship", I developed a twenty-five question survey that examined the knowledge, beliefs and understanding of 100 Christian men and women on the topic of Worship. In addition, the following five demographic questions were asked of the respondents: age, state of residence, gender, if they held an office or position in their church and if so what office or position, and how many years they have been saved. The five demographic questions were just as important as the 25 survey questions because the demographic information validated that the surveys were administered to a variety of Christians in various settings. The surveys were administered over the fall and winter of 2005-2006 to nine groups of Christian Men and Women. Groups participating in the survey included: The General Assembly of the Family Bible Ministries Worldwide, The United Missionaries of Worship International - Worship Conference, The Family Bible Ministries Seminary - Master's Candidates, The John Wesley United Methodist Church - Joshua Generation: Leadership Attendants, Workplace Settings throughout Baltimore, Maryland, Life Builders Church - Bible Study, Anointed House of Prayer, The Family Bible Ministries - Men's Bible Study, and the Men in the Life Builders Church Worship Service respectively.

B. *Summary*

The survey questions administered to 100 participants was used to substantiate the claim that there is a "Plight of Christianity for True Worship." It was designed to show a cross representation of Christian's that lack in their beliefs, knowledge and understanding of Worship. Though the survey did not support the hypothesis of ***"The Plight of Christianity for True Worship,"*** Christianity as a whole must take a closer look at the emphasis that is placed upon worship.

Worship has a direct correlation to the development and maintenance of our relationship with God. God's word declares that we were created to worship Him, as stated in John 4:23 (NIV), "But the hour cometh, and now is when the true worshippers shall worship the Father in Spirit and in truth: for the Father seeketh such to worship Him." This direction is found in the word of God. The scriptures detail when, who and how we are to worship Him. If we don't study the word of God and teach sound biblical doctrine concerning worship, the Saints of God cannot go to the next dimension of worship God is calling us to experience in Him through worship. We must now go from the outer courts, through the inner courts and into the Holy of Holies. God is looking to release us into a new realm of worship that we have yet to experience in Him. This realm is one of boldness, performing supernaturally in His Name and showing creation the manifestation of His power in the work of Worship. Worship continues to evolve," But we are with open faces beholding as in a glass, the glory of the Lord, are changed into the same image from Glory to Glory, as by the Spirit of the Lord", (2 Corinthians 3:18). Therefore, we too must evolve in our dimensions of worship." Our glorified bodies will be the final state of our perfection in worship by God.

It is time for the Saints of God to exam our common practices in worship that we consider righteous before God. We should take the example established by God in His word and consider His established pattern as the way by which we are to worship Him. He doesn't want the issue to be debated. Rather He wants us to accept His mandate unconditionally. We, the New Testament Church should reconsider the examples given to us in God's word concerning worship from the Old Testament Church. The key to worship then and now is submitting our lives to Him. God will direct us through the Holy Spirit to do what is needed in various acts of worship. Spending time with God, submitting to God, and reading His word all takes time. The scriptures declare this word by David "Bless the Lord, O my soul, and forget not all his benefits" (Psalm 103:2). Submission to God sets a precedent for believers to be blessed, their children to be blessed, and their children's children throughout eternity to be blessed. It is time for the Church of the True and Living God to rise up and personify our worship. If worshipping God is the believer's most intimately expressed celebration of our love and the value that we have for Him, then we must take it to an even greater level. God used David to reestablish worship. In the life of today's church there must be a renewed emphasis on *Music* and worship. "First - you must be committed to discovering (or rediscovering) personal worship. Second - worship must be taught, third - communicate clearly to the congregation what you are trying to do and why you are doing it, fourth - *Music* and Worship should involve the entire body of Christ." [2] Will believers submit to God to

---

[2] Vernon M. Whaley, Ph.D., <u>Understanding Music and Worship in the Local Church,</u> (Illinois: Evangelical Training Association, 1995) , 61-62

use them to reestablish His Kingdom's order of Worship? The saints of God who engage in becoming "True worshippers" no doubt pay a high price and sacrifice much for God to use us to establish Worship in His Kingdom. So did Jesus. It's not about the price that we pay, but it is about us acknowledging the price that He paid for us. For God so loved the World, that He gave His only begotten Son, that whosoever believes in Him shall not parish, but have eternal life," John 3:16.

Enter in behind the veil to Worship the King of Kings and the Lord of Lords. Let us come boldly before His throne of grace and Worship the King of Glory. Oh Magnify the Lord with me. Let us Exalt His name together. He is everything lovely and He is my pure delight. He is perfect in all His ways. When I consider the Heavens and the works of thy hands, I cry out -- Holy, Holy, Holy is the Lord God Almighty. Blessed be His Holy Name.

Chapter 3:

"In Spirit and in Truth"

Chapter 3: "In Spirit and in Truth"

I Defining Worship

A. Introduction

From the beginning of creation God established worship as ***the means by which humanity expresses their abiding love and appreciation for God and celebrate how much we value a personal and intimate relationship with Him***. Not only do we worship the Lord God, but all of the Heavenly Host and Angels worship God. In order to worship God, we must come to the full realization of the definition, purpose, forms, work, order and benefits of Worship. In addition, we must understand the difference between active and passive worship, have a biblical understanding that Jesus worshipped His Father, as well as know the impact of True Worshippers on the Kingdom of God. Throughout this section entitled "In Spirit and In Truth", these previously mentioned biblical truths on worship will be discussed. As stated previously, the answer to "The Plight of Christianity for True worship" is for Christians to study the word of God and take responsibility for teaching sound biblical doctrine concerning Worship, which is the intent of the preceding pages. The teachings in this book will give the believer greater biblical knowledge on "Worship", and it is written in a form for the new believer and for the seasoned saint to learn biblical truths concerning "Worship."

The first thing that we must do in order to study worship is to define what it is. To many it may be difficult to describe worship however; through the use of many resources a definition has been established. The Greek word for worship is in the form of a verb "***proskuneo***", meaning to prostrate one's self in homage (do reverence to, adore). Vine's Complete Expository Dictionary notes that the worship of God is no where defined in Scripture. It may be regarded as the direct acknowledgment to God, of His nature, attributes, ways and claims, whether by the outgoing of the heart in praise and thanksgiving or by deed done in such acknowledgement. The Old Testament word for Worship is **Shachah**: prostrate, beseech humbly; related to an attitude; involves the stretching out of the hands towards God or bending of the knee. Simply stated again, ***"True Worship of God is the means by which humanity expresses their abiding love and appreciation for God and celebrate how much we value a personal and intimate relationship with Him***.

There is often a misconception of the definition of worship. Some believers confuse the definition of worship with the definition of praise. Some believers use the words praise and worship synonymously when they are in fact clearly different. Worship is the celebration of our value for God. When we think of worship we must think of our love for God and also consider our Worth-ship of Him or His worth to us. In thinking of worth, we must regard the value of the God of all wonders seated on His throne of Majesty. How much do we really value God? In what ways do we value His abiding love? Do we value His faithfulness? Do we value His abilities "to do exceeding abundantly above all that we ask or think according to the power that worketh in us", (Ephesians 3:20). All of these points should be considered when we express our Worship of God.

Praise on the other hand, is a word that is said in conjunction with worship, however, they are not one in the same. Praise is our formal expression of thankfulness for the deeds that God has done, is doing and will do on our behalf. From a grateful heart we tell God how much we are thankful for everything He has done for us, through us, and with us down to the most minute of details. When the Saints of God praise, "it is the act of bragging on God." An understanding of Praise and Worship is absolutely essential if we are to take our place in the New Testament church." [3] We Praise God knowing "For my thoughts are not your thoughts, neither are your ways my ways declares the Lord" (Isaiah 55:8). Blessed be His Holy Name. We are to Praise God in all situations, good or bad. Praise unlocks a door in the Heavenlies. Worship establishes God's Kingdom here on earth. "An understanding of Praise and Worship is absolutely essential if we are to take our place in the New Testament church". [4]

B. Relationship

Worship is our response to a relationship with God. On the relational level, worship expresses how we celebrate our relationship with God as our Father, Savior, Lord, Lover of our Soul, Provider, Protector, Enabler, Righteousness, Perfector, and Creator of all Creation. Our worship is expressed based upon our relationship. "Worship is rejoicing in the fact that God is your Friend, Redeemer, Comforter, Companion, Sovereign, Provider, Healer, Giver of Life and Peace." [5] He is called "Abba"

---

[3] Pastor Rod Parsley with Clint Brown, Praise the Ultimate Experience - Worship the Ultimate Relationship, (Ohio: Results Publishing, 1992), 15.

[4] Pastor Rod Parsley with Clint Brown, Praise the Ultimate Experience - Worship the Ultimate Relationship, (Ohio: Results Publishing, 1992), 18.

[5] Vernon Whaley, Ph.D., Understanding Music and Worship in the Local Church, (Illinois: Evangelical Training Association, 2002) 15.

Father - as we relate to Him as "our Father" who watches over us. We call Him the Breasted One as He beckons us to lay and be at rest. On a personal basis He continues to be my Mediator, Counselor and Teacher. Who He is to us is based upon the relationship that we have with Him. Only through relationship do we know Him in these intimate ways. And He - the Sovereign Lord will manifest Himself in these ways. How can we call upon Him unless we have an intimate relationship with Him? An intimate relationship is not developed with God through our crying out in times of stress, duress, struggles or trials. The development of an intimate relationship comes from just spending time with God. Not just when we pray but when we spend time in prayer. It is in prayer that God will "tell us the great and unsearchable things we do not know", (Jeremiah 33:3), and we in turn have an outpouring of our inner thoughts towards God.

A pattern of intimate relationships between God and His children are shown throughout the Bible. Remember David - a man after God's own heart, through relationship in the 2nd letter of Samuel in Chapter 7 - God made a covenant with David to bless his seed, grant David's son the ability to build God's temple, as well as establish an eternal dynasty as a result of obedience. Because of relationship, God sent Angels to remove Lot and his whole family from catastrophe at Sodom and Gomorra according to the 19th chapter in Genesis. A relationship with God establishes His word. He says "The Lord will fulfill his purpose for me" (Psalm 138:8). Through relationship, God's word in Malachi 3:10-12 declares promises of abundance. Furthermore, through relationship, God so loved the world that He gave His one and only son that whosoever believeth in Him shall not perish but have eternal life, John 3:16. Because of relationship God selected Mary to be the mother of Jesus and bring forth the Messiah as indicated in

Luke 1:26-35. Do you see how God has established a multitude of blessings for those who have come into a covenant relationship and Worship Him? There really is a benefit of establishing a relationship with God, through Worship.

Worship is a lifestyle and not a ritualistic practice. It is by no means a religious practice and we certainly don't worship just because we feel like it. Adapting a lifestyle of worship means that we continuously celebrate and express our value for God known as "Worthship." Worth-ship means to ascribe how much we sincerely value Him. It goes beyond acknowledging and expressing who God is at the beginning, middle, day and even at the end of our day. If we really sought to count the times that we acknowledged God it would be innumerable. With a lifestyle of worship the Saints of God boldly proclaim that "His praise will always be on my lips", Psalms 34:1 and continuously express how much we value the only True and Living God.

C. Expression

In worship the children of God express their celebration and value of God. We express audibly and we also express in physical manifestations. Our audible expressions are defined as such because it is heard. We hear it as we express it, Heavenly Hosts hear our expressions and most importantly, Almighty God hears our expressions. Our audible expressions come in a form of language that we can identify with because it is our normal language. However, we also have a "love language" that comes in the form of an unknown language known as "Tongues." The manifestation of this gift is subject to the Holy Spirit. The Spirit himself intercedes for us with groans that words cannot express. Individual Styles of Expression manifested in worship will be covered later in this chapter.

D. *In Spirit and in Truth*

God's word declared in the Gospel of John 4:23 states, "But the hour cometh, and now is when the true worshippers shall worship the Father in Spirit and in Truth: for the Father seeketh such to worship Him (NIV). In order to understand worship, we must fully understand what it means to worship "In Spirit and In Truth." As previously stated *"True Worship of God is the means by which humanity expresses their abiding love and appreciation for God and celebrate how much we value a personal and intimate relationship with Him*." If worship is to be effective, it must be spiritual in nature." [6] God created every believer with a human spirit by which he or she can communicate with the Spirit of God. When we come before the throne of grace it is by the human spirit that we worship Almighty God." Genuine worship that pleases God operates in the realm of truth--the true knowledge of God."[7] The Saints of God who worship in spirit and truth are not defined by ethical truth or integrity of character nor through being faithful or genuine. These truths are manifested in the lives of the believers who read God's truths in His word, and are lead in these truths by the Holy Spirit. To "Worship in Spirit and Truth is worship that is focused on the risen, exalted Christ and empowered by

---

[6] John Rea, Th.D. , <u>Charisma's Bible Handbook on the Holy Spirit</u>, Florida: Creation House, 1998) 130.

[7] John Rea, Th.D. , <u>Charisma's Bible Handbook on the Holy Spirit</u>, (Florida: Creation House, 1998)

His Spirit."[8] The combination of these components is absolutely necessary to establish God's Kingdom on earth, as we extol and magnify the Holy God who has created us with a privilege to worship Him. "When you turn your heart toward God with no hypocrisy or deceit, true worship will take place." [9]

II.   The Purpose of Worship

The believer in Christ worships the True and Living God for the following reasons: First, it is a command in God's word according to John 4:23. Second, it is why the creator of all living things created us. Third, it is necessary to establish the Kingdom of God. Lastly, through participating in worship, we are being prepared to receive the word of God. As we study the scripture in John 4:23, God reveals Himself and His purpose for us. Described in this scripture is a command that we must acknowledge and accept this mandate as our personal direction from God. There is no room for an option. Every believer in Christ has been created by the outstretched hands of Almighty God. It is imperative that we do not compromise the reason by which we were created and that is to worship the Most High God.

Through worship we set the atmosphere for the sovereign abilities of God to be manifested. As believers in God we have the opportunity and privilege to express the nature of our personal relationship with God and how much

---

[8] John Rea, Th.D. , <u>Charisma's Bible Handbook on the Holy Spirit</u>, (Florida: Creation House, 1998) 130.

[9] Vernon M. Whalen, Ph.D., <u>Understanding Music and Worship in the Local Church,</u> (Illinois: Evangelical Training Association, 2002) 10.

we value His sovereignty to be all, do all, know all, and to have His will be done. God's Kingdom is so complex, that we cannot fathom the complexities of His infinite power. However, we do know God's abilities through experience-ing his power on a personal basis. In worship, God's abilities are established and manifested. It is here that we touch the hem of His garment and become whole and no longer broken. Many saints of the Most High God do not understand that worship brings transformation of lives through healing and deliverance from physical disease, spiritual oppression, depression, temptation, relational difficulties, financial bondage, and other forms of domination. But most important, worship prepares the body of Christ to receive the word of God. In worship we are emptied of ourselves. Our mind, body and spirit are being readied to hear the voice of the Lord to bear witness to the manifestation of His Mercy. Worship and an intimate relationship with God allow us to be able to exist in this world by applying God's word to live the abundant life that God has promised.

III.   Forms of Worship: Singing- Dancing- Playing Instruments

Just as there are many members in the body of Christ, there are many churches in the body of Christ that conduct various forms of worship. As we study these various forms of worship we will exam their origins and biblical significance. Keep in mind that Christians must have the right motives and serve in these various capacities with thankfulness to exalt God in these various forms of worship.

A. *Singing*

The first form of worship I will address are the people who make music with their voices. The Hebrew word Ranan "occurs approximately 50 times in the Hebrew Old Testament,"[10] which means "to shout or cry out" and is often used to express joy and exultation." In the Old and New Testament there were many accounts of worship assemblies that included Levitical singers - female as well as male, and choirs in the temple. These instruments of worship sang from the depths of their hearts to extol and magnify God. 1 Chronicles 15: 22-26 states, "Kenaniah the head Levite was in charge of the singing; that was his responsibility because he was skillful at it." And in verse 27 it states that they were clothed in a robe of fine linen. This scripture suggests that there were some men and women believers who were assigned and trained by God to sing in the courts of the Most High. Therefore, they were skilled and held accountable to someone to minister under the anointing of God in excellence. Singing in the Old Testament and even now during worship is not just for the trained members of the inner court. According to Ephesians 5:19-20 all Christians are admonished by God to, "Speak to one another with psalms, hymns and spiritual songs. Sing and make music in your heart to the Lord, always giving thanks to God the Father for everything, in the name of our Lord Jesus Christ." Scriptures' detail accounts of the saints singing unto God concerning thanksgiving, gladness, power, mercy, righteousness, and His grace

Worship in the form of singing occurred before battles,

---

[10] W.E. Vine, <u>Vine's Complete Expository Dictionary of Old and New Testament Words,</u> Tennessee: Thomas Nelson, Inc., 1996) 234.

after victories were won, in jubilation and in sorrow. An account in Acts 16:25-26 states that, "About midnight Paul and Silas were praying and singing hymns to God, and the other prisoners were listening to them." When the Saints of God sing unto the Lord in worship, they activate power in the heavenlies. Likewise, we draw men unto God because of the power that is activated here on earth.

Singing by all accounts is a gift from God to His people, for His good pleasure. Through singing, we minister to God. He listens not just to the words we speak in song but also to the intent or the motive of our heart. He doesn't want the believer to speak life into the atmosphere and not have the intent of our heart aligned to awaken the lifeless through our praise. In 1 Corinthians 14:15 the scripture gives us the depths of the understanding of God during the Old Testament regarding the intent of the heart during worship, "I will pray with my spirit, but I will also sing with my mind." Evidenced here in the scripture, God sees the true intent of our heart as we worship through singing.

B. *Minstrels*

<u>Musicians</u>

God's chosen people who play a musical instrument during worship are known as minstrels and requires a special anointing from God. Minstrels or instrumentalists in the body of Christ have a position that is not to be taken lightly, for they have been chosen to usher in the presence of God. "There is a special anointing that accompanies instruments, often bring in a tangible anointing of the presence of God and allowing me to hear the direction of

God for the service."[11] Musicians minister to God and set the atmosphere of worship. Therefore, their motives, which are to glorify God, must be pure. God anointed King David with wisdom to organize worship according to 1 Chronicles 15:19-22, and established a precedence to hold musicians accountable to those designated in authority for the performance of music in the sanctuary. It was not enough that they were anointed to play a musical instrument, they had to practice as well. "King David organized music and worship with formal guidelines for the education, training, and employment of musicians for the House of God."[12]

Often times the Saints of God become inspired to sing or speak under the anointing of music. Psalm 144:1 states: "Praise be to the Lord my Rock, who trains my hands for war, my fingers for battle." This scripture implies that those who are anointed to play musical instruments use their fingers to war in the spirit realm. These anointed musicians use instruments to ring forth sounds in the spirit realm that cannot be heard or understood in the natural but have supernatural significance and perform supernatural task. Musicians play at worship services, farewells, weddings, funerals, sacred processionals, victory celebrations, and dedications.

Instruments

In worship, according to Psalm 33:3 we are to,

---

[11] Pastor Rod Parsley with Clint Brown, <u>Praise the Ultimate Experience Worship the Ultimate Relationship,</u> (Ohio: Results Publishing, 1992) 55.

[12] Vernon M. Whaley, Ph. D., <u>Understanding Music & Worship in the Local Church</u>, (Illinois: Evangelical Training Association, 2002) 35.

"Sing to Him a new song; play skillfully, and shout for joy." This charge was given to the anointed of God to play music in the sanctuary. In the Psalms, David notes the various instruments that were used during worship services in the Old Testament and specifically declares in Psalm 150: 3-5, "Praise Him with the sounding of the trumpet, praise Him with the harp and lyre, praise Him with tambourine and dancing, praise Him with the strings and flute, praise Him with the clash of cymbals, praise Him with resounding cymbals." Other Old Testament instruments included the Harp, Cymbals, and Psalter. Playing musical instruments can be conducted by all genders. Exodus 15:20 states, "Then Miriam the prophetess, Aaron's sister took a tambourine in her hand, and all the women followed her, with tambourines and dancing." The anointed playing of musical instruments is used to inspire and soothe the heart of man. Take for instance in 1 Samuel 16: 23, "Whenever the spirit from God came upon Saul, David would take his harp and play. Then relief would come to Saul; he would feel better and the evil sprit would leave him."

C. Dancing

The ministry of dance existed throughout the entire Old Testament and continues to exist throughout the New Testament church today. The Hebrew word for dance is *orcheo* which means to lift up," as of the feet; hence "to leap with regularity of motion."[13] Whether performing as

---

[13] W. E. Vine, Vine's Complete Expository Dictionary of Old and New Testament Words with Topical Index, (Tennessee: Thomas Nelson Publishers, 1996).

an individual or in a dance company know in Hebrew as "*Mekholaw*", recognize that dancing is a Holy ministry. Those called into this ministry are not only appointed but also trained to perfect this gift. These dancers portray an expression of the inner man through rhythmic stepping coordinated to the beat of music. In worship, a dancer receives spirit lead movements from God to relay to the congregation, which cannot be verbally articulated. They proclaim the work of God and direct people to visualize what He is doing in the heavenlies that are now being released on earth. Significant power is released in worship through dance and it in turn releases expressions of rejoicing and revelation of pitfalls set by the enemy whose strongholds are destroyed. Psalm 30:11 reveals this power, "You turned my wailing into dancing; you removed my sackcloth and clothed me with joy." Participation in the visualization of dance is a privilege for the believers to receive the manifestation of the power released in worship. Dance performances are not just conducted by women, children and men. 2 Sam 6:14 details a King, one of the greatest worshippers of all time dancing, "David, wearing a linen ephod, danced before the Lord with all his might."

IV. Individual Styles of Expressions in Worship

Christians worship God as a result of an individual personal relationship with Him. So it is also that God has given each of us individual styles of expression in worship. To some, our individual style of worship may seem strange, because it is not the traditional way in which they are accustomed. However, God uses each style of worship to make an impact upon the spirit realm. As we review some of the various forms of expression in worship, the reader will get a better understanding of their purposes as they are manifested in worship. Some of these unique expressions in worship use our bodies, for instance when we stomp. In other styles of worship additional resources are used to worship such as the waving of banners in our hands. As unique as these expressions in worship may appear, they all have biblical and spiritual significance that will be discussed herein.

Moreover, the one thing that remains constant in these expressions is the fact that the Holy Spirit Himself directs us in worship, to do the will of God. The Spirit of God reveals spiritual truths during worship that the human mind cannot fully comprehend or direct. Man cannot orchestrate nor can he direct the symbolic representations that are manifested in these individual expressions of worship. But we must trust in God to know that He has a purpose for every expression. The timing of synchronized clapping of the corporate body, the full force of the saints jumping up and down, the man laying prostrate before the altar, and the woman lifting her hands into the air shouting "Holy, Holy, Holy is the Lord God Almighty" are all orchestrated with a divine purpose. This purpose is to release the power of God by penetrating the heavenlies, to impact individuals and the corporate body of Christ. Most of all these expressions of worship are for the glorification of God.

A. Clapping Hands

Macha is the Hebrew word for clap, which means to strike the hands together. Psalm 47:1: directs us to clap your hands, all you nations; shout to God with cries of joy." This scripture reveals a direction from God to clap our hands but also for us to know that there is a triumphant purpose being performed when we yield and act according to the will of God. Once we have clapped according to the Hebrew word **_Nakah,_** God will, kill, make slaughter, punish, slay, smite, and stricken the works of the enemy. During worship some of God's people are given the assignment of walking through the sanctuary clapping their hands. It is through performing this expression during worship that God overthrows the works of satan, the defeated foe. Clapping is like releasing the sound of thunder, which brings fear against the powers of wickedness.

B. Shouting

Shouting in the sanctuary is not an uncommon expression during worship. This form of expression is sometimes thought of as distracting. It includes those that speak or sing unto the Lord in a loud tone. Those who are lead to move in this dimension of the anointing of God are called to release a powerful spiritual significance. Ezekiel 21:22 states, "to give the command to slaughter, <u>to sound the battle cry</u>, to set battering rams against the gates, to build a ramp and to erect siege works." In Isaiah 12:5 we are admonished to "Shout aloud and sing for joy, people of Zion, for great is the Holy One of Israel among you." Shouting has several meanings such as to acclaim, call for help, to sound, or battle cry, they all have the same effect. When one shouts under the anointing of God they let out a battle cry which cancels the effects of satan.

C. Waving Banners

In some congregations multi-colored banners are waved during the worship service. The waving of these banners indicate the defeat of the enemy. It is the blood stained banner of Jesus Christ being waved signifying His covering and protection in the face of the enemy during spiritual warfare. When Moses raised the banner before Israel and it was maintained in an upright position, they remained triumphant. A major lesson was taught to the people of Israel that when they fought in the strength of God they were always victorious. Waving a banner is symbolic of God's omniscience and omnipresence.

D. Kneeling

Kneeling during worship is used as an act of humble submission to bless God through adoration of His sovereignty and love. The Scriptures in Daniel 6:10 reveal, "Now when Daniel learned that the decree had been published, he went home to his upstairs room where the windows opened toward Jerusalem. Three times a day, he got down on his knees and prayed, giving thanks to his God, just as he had done before." The Hebrew word ***"Barak"*** is emphasized here as Daniel worshipped God and spoke well of Him. Though we recognize that it is an honor and privilege to come before the Great I AM, we must also recognize that "True Worship" will bring out our true adoration and affection for God. Therefore, we kneel before Him and honor the Lord.

E. Bowing

Paul writes In Romans 14:11, "It is written: As surely as I live, says the Lord, every knee will bow before me; every tongue will confess to God." In Psalm 95:6 the author directs us to "Come, let us bow down in worship, let us kneel before the Lord our Maker." The significance of bowing in both of these scriptures is meant for us to yield ourselves before God acknowledging and reverencing Him. When we bow before God, it is an intentional act of submission that we bend or turn from our abilities and look toward God's abilities.

F. Laying Prostrate

To witness men, women and/or even children lying prostrate on the floor may seem peculiar to some. However, this act of expression in worship should be considered common. To prostrate oneself means that we are devoting ourselves to God. In 2 Kings 17:36 the author writes, "But the Lord, who brought you up out of Egypt with mighty power and outstretched arm, is the one you must worship." There is no question here as to what we are to do and to whom we are to do it. We are to devote ourselves in worship to God. The act of laying prostate in devotion must be directed towards God.

G. Lifting up out-stretched hands

Lifting outstretched hands in the sanctuary is symbolic of releasing one's own abilities and surrendering our will unto God. Genesis 14:22 states, "But Abraham said to the king of Sodom, "I have raised my hand to the Lord, God Most High, Creator of Heaven and earth, and have taken an oath." In this scripture Abraham grasped the concept that the present state of his particular circumstance was totally out of his control. When we lift our hands according to Psalms 134:2 "Lift up your hands in the sanctuary and praise the Lord", we are acknowledging, accepting, and surrendering our problems and circumstances to God. During the struggles of our lives, the battles are won through obediently lifting holy hands towards God.

H. Speaking

God's word is shared among His people in worship. Among the people of God there are many gifts that are administered by speaking, other than that of the preacher or teacher. God has chosen and anointed some to speak on His behalf, to minister in the prophetic gift, and/or to edify the body of Christ. As the spirit gives utterance to the prophet they will either foretell or forthtell the will of God.

Another spoken style of expression in worship is shouting. The Hebrew word for shouting is Halel which means to get foolish for God by boasting in celebration, or raving about God. God's people can be observed loudly proclaiming the blessings, grace and mercy of God in worship. Psalm 34:1 declares, "I will extol the Lord at all times; His praise will always be on my lips." Though we often hear the loud exaltations spoken throughout the sanctuary, it is good to know that this too has a meaning.

There are so many other individual styles of expressions in worship that have not been discussed and some that have yet to be revealed. But what Christians must remember is that in "True Worship", the manifestation of these expressions will only come from the Holy Spirit and through a vessel willing to be used by the Master. The manifestation of these expressions is not limited to gender, age, or specific gifting. God will anoint and use those persons that are open for Him to perform a work through. When we freely give ourselves to God, then He will "tell you the great and unsearchable things you do not know", according to Jeremiah 33:11. There are no works of the flesh that can conduct the manifestation of these styles of expressions in worship and produce spiritual significance. Know that they are for God's Glory. He has established and purposely designed each one of these expressions in worship for the edification of the Body of Christ. Willing vessels are not limited to how these expressions are manifested. The only limits in worship are self-imposed by man. Now that the revelation behind these spiritual manifestations has been illuminated, we must consider the impact of these individual styles of expressions in worship upon our lives individually and corporately upon the Kingdom of God. There is an ultimate purpose to each one of these individual expressions demonstrated in worship.

V.   The Work of Worship

When we *"Enter into His gates with thanksgiving and into His courts with praise. Be thankful to Him, and bless His name"* (Psalms 100:4), God looks upon us sovereignly. It is at that very moment that He releases His steadfast power from the heavenlies upon His Kingdom on the Earth. We may think entering into His gates to worship is demonstrated when we enter into the sanctuaries of our choice, but Worship as it has been defined, can take place outside of the constructed walls of the church and be demonstrated in our homes or places where God has instructed us to build an alter on His behalf. This altar is a place of surrender where the focus is removed from one's self and it is placed upon God. Worship is personal and the impact of our participation produces a spiritual work that cannot be conducted by a mere man. Just as worship has it's various individual expressions, so too does worship have its various works. The hand of the Almighty God infinitely performs these works. God gives man the privilege to worship. We enter this secret place to express the magnitude of God's significance in our lives. He beckons all of His people to enter in to the place of rest where He unveils His promise that *"you will we seek Me and find Me when you seek Me with all your heart,"* Jeremiah 29:13. Seeking God through worship is the pathway by which the work is done on our behalf. When we seek after God and find Him it means that we participate in experiencing God through relationship. Through this relationship we have the privilege to know the Creator of All Things. This same

Creator has created us to worship Him. Likewise, the same one who has created us to worship Him, will perform the work of worship. We assume that we can attest to know God to heal, deliver, provide, bless, direct, fight, and to do so much more. However, for the purpose contained herein we will discuss how the work God performed in worship, is in direct correlation to who we esteem God to be, through our personal relationship with Him.

In worship God performs a spiritual work in man's heart, spirit, and soul; conducts restoration; goes to war against principalities and spiritual wickedness, releases blessings, causes His word to come to pass, sends forth His power, and shows us the significance of His love. In order to execute all of this work, it requires the conduction of miracles from a supernatural being, which is God. The prerequisite to the release of these miracles is worship. God requires man to worship. He will not entrust His treasures with those that do not love, serve and worship Him. The more we worship Him, the more intense God works on our behalf and the more intimate our relation-ship with Him becomes. God's infinite power through worship "is able to do exceedingly abundantly above all that we ask or think according to the power that works in us" (Ephesians 3:20). When we personalize our relation-ship with God through intimate worship, we experience all of these things and so much more. Through worship, God performs the work of Jehovah-Elohim-creator of all things, self-existent one. Jehovah Elohim, the creator of all creation shows us how in the middle of a major drought that, "I will even make a road in the wilderness And rivers in the desert " according to Isaiah 43:19. Even in these places God will restore, refresh, and sustains those that believe in Him.

It is in Worship where God invites us to experience _Jehovah-shalom,_ the God of Peace. During worship, His work gives "the Peace of God which surpasses all understanding, will guard your hearts and minds in Christ Jesus," Philippians 4:7. The work of Jehovah-shalom in worship releases us from oppression, depression, bondage, confinement, and affliction. After this work is completed, we will be able to say, "So if the son makes you free, you should be free indeed", John 8:36, because of personal experience.

Resting in the work of Jehovah-shalom, God subtly shows us the work of Jehovah-Nissi, the Lord our Banner. His work consists of conquering the enemy satan. Jehovah-Nissi lifts up the blood stained banner of Jesus Christ and goes before us in battle. Spiritual weapons are launched and He strategizes against Satan. God's word in 2 Corinthians 10:4-5 states "For the weapons of our warfare are not carnal, but mighty in God for pulling down strongholds, casting down arguments and every high thing that exaluts itself against the knowledge of God, bringing every thought into captivity to the obedience of Christ." "For we do not wrestle against flesh and blood, but against principalities, against powers, against the rulers of the darkness of this age, against spiritual hosts of wickedness in the heavenly places." (Ephesians 6:12). The warrior Jehovah-Nissi releases the Word of God and the blood of Jesus over every circumstance being released upon us to destroy us. Individually and collectively all three release power, cleanse; refresh; give victory, and take authority over God's Kingdom. Jehovah-Nissi proves time and time again that satan is a defeated foe.

Jehovah-Tsidkenu, the Lord our righteousness works on our behalf during worship to help us maintain our righteousness before God. Because we were born into sin we need Jehovah-Tsidkenu to justify us, cleanse us, and purify our motives. Psalm 51:10 states, "Create in me a pure heart, O God, and renew a steadfast spirit within me." Thereby enabling us to come before a Holy God as a Holy people for a Holy work.

As the Healer, Jehovah-Rophe conducts the work of spiritual surgery. His work of healing includes making the heart, mind, soul and body whole. In this work of worship Jehovah-Rophe pronounces and declares "Is there anything too hard for the Lord", Genesis 18:4. Jehovah-Rophe destroys yolks and lifts burdens, afflictions, impediments, disappointments, crushed dreams, and ill effects of circumstances that have plagued the lives of God's people. "Therefore if anyone is in Christ, he is a new Creation; old things have passed away; behold, all things have become new", 2 Corinthians 5:17.

The work of the Almighty One-El Shaddai, our source of comfort and strength is crucial during worship. El Shaddai manifests God's promise that "His strength is made perfect in our weakness". Man cannot do His work. His capabilities are supernatural, in that man is incapable of doing what the Almighty one can do. The weaker we are, the greater "El Shaddai - the Almighty One."

Worshipping releases "increase" through the power of Jehovah-Jireh, it shall be provided. In worship the wants and needs of the people of God are established and given through the work of Jehovah Jireh. God's steadfast faithfulness is made known and the provisions for His Kingdom are released. His word declares "God has planned (provided) something better for us that they should not be made perfect apart from us according to, " Hebrews 11:40.

God's word declares that "I will never leave you nor forsake you", as stated in Hebrews 13:5. This scripture is where the work of Jehovah-Shammah in worship is manifested. The feelings of being alone and loneliness are fought on our behalf. In its place, the presence of God, in all that we do becomes greater. We see that He is all and in all that we do. The steps we walk are purposed and we are not alone as we worship.

The children of God by nature are prone to wander and need the work of Jehovah-Rohi in worship. The Good Shepherd-Jehovah Rohi functions in directing God's children in the many pathways of their lives. His leadership function reveals the role of Jehovah-Rohi in Psalm 23:1-3,"The Lord is my Shepherd I shall not want. He makes me to lie down in green pastures, He leads me beside the still waters, and He restores my soul. He leads me in paths of righteousness for His name's sake," **He leads His flock, points the way, and gives the route for destiny to be apprehended.**" Had it not been for the work of Jehovah-Rohi in worship, we would be lost.

The person of God that we experience in worship manifests His abilities to work on our behalf, as a result of our relationship with Him. Just some of the divine natures of God are listed here that show the manifold abilities of "the works of your (God's) hands" Psalm 92:4. Keep in mind that the whole essence of our being connected with God is relational. Therefore, without a relationship we cannot have expectancy for any of the sovereign powers of God to move on our behalf. His abilities however are infinite. All of God's abilities can be experienced by all of His people. We should come into worship with expectancy in our heart for the manifestation of the work of God's hands.

The work that God conducts in worship should not be taken lightly. We cannot assume that it will be done. But we must actively participate in the worship experience as well as anticipate a move of God to take place first in the heavenlies and then here on earth. God sovereignly tells us "and we know that in all things God works for the good of those who love him, who have been called according to his purpose", Roman 8:28. These works are conducted in and through worship.

VI. God's Order of Worship

A. Order

The order of worship has been given to us in the word of God. Its established pattern transcends through-out history and the scriptures overflow with direction on worship. Several of these scriptures will now be examined. Let's begin in Exodus 34:14 where the word of God declares "for you shall worship no other god, for the Lord, whose name is Jealous, is a jealous God." This scripture is a warning to God's people of His resentment of idolatry. In Deuteronomy 26:10 the posture of worship is detailed in the following, we are to "Place the basket before the Lord your God and bow down before him." Bowing down is symbolic of the humble submission of God's children to a Holy God. The direction in 1 Chronicles 16:29 charges every believer to "worship the Lord in the splendor of his Holiness."

When God's brilliance is displayed throughout the heavens it is at this very time that we are to worship. God does not discount anyone that should worship him as revealed in Psalms 66:4, "All the earth bows down to you; they sing praise to you, they sing praise to your name." Matthew 4:10 "Jesus said to him, " Away from me Satan. For it is written: Worship the Lord your God, and serve Him only. This scripture from the New Testament makes a bold statement that God Himself is the only one to be worshipped.

In the scripture references above, we have stated some of the order of worship that God has given to the believer including who not to worship, a posture of worship, when worship should be conducted, and who to worship. Through reading the Bible and being lead by the Holy Spirit believers will find so many more emphasis that God has given concerning the order of worship.

Worship is not limited by time. Its relevance is not conditional to the state of being of man. The order of worship is how God has ordained its time, season, the manifestation of His presence, the persons participating in worship, and how they manifest their expressions of worship. "The time is coming when the Body of Christ will know how to release themselves in worship to God. His presence will be manifested in such a way that people are going to receive miracles--legs are going to be straightened, blind eyes are going to be opened, the lame are going to walk -- without anybody praying for them or laying hands on them. [14] This manifestation is God's order of worship.

God is concerned about the intent of man's heart in worship. As previously stated, He wants our worship to be free and uninhibited. He is not concerned about the order of man directing His worship line by line. God wants to set the stage for the production of His work, the manifestation of His gifts, even down to how He is presented on His throne. Worship is a perfect example of God's self-rule. Man cannot take out his day planner, schedule a date, direct every scene to occur, place people in a particular position

---

[14] Pastor Rod Parsley with Clint Brown, <u>Praise the Ultimate Experience Worship the Ultimate Relationship</u>, (Ohio: Results Publishing, 1992) 66.

to complete a task or establish their own agenda for God's worship service. The worship service was created by God, for God.

B. *Corporate Worship*

As we examine God's order of worship, it is just as important to emphasize corporate worship. Recall the story in Acts 2:1, "when the day of Pentecost came, they were all together <u>in one place</u>." The Lord shows in this scripture the importance of being in the right place, being in agreement with the people in that place, and the power of unity. When the Saints of God pursue a divine assignment, the manifold blessings overflow into the sanctuary and overtake everyone on one accord. Corporate worship promotes this same impact. God's people worship Him corporately and the manifestations that God has designed to spring forth in worship is received by all in the worship service. The manifestations in worship are different for each member in the body of Christ. However, the impact and significance of the manifestations are at the same level of distribution. This manifestation comes through obedience. In order for the impact to be fully realized the entire body of Christ is required to be standing in agreement in worship in their local assembly. A greater sacrifice is required from a corporate body because a greater reward is given for the corporate body as a whole. The entire body including children is to follow the direction of leadership in worship. It doesn't matter if we are being lead to clap our hands, bow, sing, dance, jump up and down or shout. Corporate unity is required of the Body of Christ in corporate worship. The word of God declared in Psalm 133: states, "How good and pleasant it is when brethren live together in unity. This same unity applies to every facet of the life of the believer, even in worship. God says it is "good and pleasant." We should participate in corporate worship for no other reason but that the lover of our soul tells us to do so and we desire to be obedient.

VII. The Benefits of Worship

It is difficult to pinpoint the direct benefit of worship because of God's sovereignty and infinite abilities. In worship we should anticipate a move of God. But the reality is that God's power, dominion and authority are subject to His sovereignty. Just because we cry out to the only True and Living God, sacrifice time, humble ourselves, submit our will unto Him, extol Him with words that cannot describe or measure His greatness in worship, does not mean that we will receive anything from God. It is only because of His sovereign will that we experience the move of God's hand during worship.

In the natural sense, most people believe that if they give something, they will receive something. But in the spiritual realm, we serve a God whose sovereign ability will make the final determination of the outpouring of His blessings in worship. As His divine will is structured for our lives, then it is unto us to have His blessings. The greatest expectation in worship is that God arises and our enemies are defeated. In worship, God reigns down upon us in victory, power, and strength. He sets aside strategic maneuvers to ensnare the enemy and loose the chains that bind us, with abilities far greater than our own.

In worship it is not so much that we seek after a benefit from God. By virtue of who God is, in worship, we find that He is the benefit. His present to us in worship is His presence. The scriptures declare that we are to "Worship the Lord in the splendor of His Holiness" (1Chronicles 16:29). God's Holiness is experienced through worship. Consider for a moment a worship experience in the presence of the Most High God. Believers are in an atmosphere saturated with the presence of God. To most believers this experience is absolutely indescribable. There is no measurable value to this benefit and privilege. Holiness is beautiful, pure, uncorrupted, uncontaminated, genuine, virtuous, upright, honorable, righteous, and just. This intangible gift is what is presented to us, when the Body of Christ come before Almighty God and "offer your bodies as living sacrifices, holy and pleasing to God-this is your spiritual act of worship", (Romans 12:1). Unmistakably, there are innumerable benefits for worshipping the Most High God. Our greatest gain is the relationship with the Lord Jesus Christ. The scriptures tell us that "I have come that they may have life, and have it to the full" (John 10:10). He also promised in His word "For the wages of sin is death, but the gift of God is eternal life in Christ Jesus our Lord (Romans 6:23). As a True Worshipper of God we must not look for the benefit of worship more than we look for the giver of the benefits in worship, our Lord and Savior Jesus Christ.

VIII. Active verses Passive Worship

In today's church there are some Christians that are active and some that are passive in their approach to worship. The active participants are seen moving in the will of God, alive and free, operating in the gifts of God, and enthusiastic about the presence of our unseen God. On the other hand, passive participants are inactive in the assembly of God's people, insensitive to the spirit of God, rendering themselves motionless, inattentive to God's direction, and listless. My question to the saints of the Most High God is "where do you see yourselves as worshippers? Passive or Active"? "Jesus reminded the Samaritan woman, and reminds us, worship is first and foremost a spiritual activity."15 One cannot worship in a stationary posture. A vital component to worship is submission and rendering of oneself to God. These components can be seen from the natural eye, but the true expression is conducted in the spirit. Active worship is performed in the spirit where our spirit aligns with the spirit of God. Active worship also requires unity. Psalms 133:1 declares, "How good and pleasant it is when brothers live together in unity!" This unity is the active approach to worship. It is what God is calling the church to do. When leadership tells us to actively participate in worship by raising our hands and bowing as a body, we are to do so. God is not and will never be pleased with partial participation. It would mean that we partially love the Lord, which is unacceptable.

---

15 Vernon M. Whaley, Ph.D., <u>Understanding Music and Worship in the Local Church,</u> Evangelical Training Association, 2002, pg. 10.

IX. Create a Habitation for True Worship

The order of worship established in the Old Testament instructs us to create a tabernacle or a place of habitation for worship. Habitation is defined in Webster's Pocket dictionary as a dwelling. To biblically define habitation I will use the Hebrew words *katoiketerion* (which means dwelling-place, home) and *katoikia* (which means residence, dwelling). When we create a habitation we are to create a dwelling-place, home, or residence for God. This dwelling-place is not just a physical space. It is more of a spiritual connection linking one's state-of-mind, body, and spirit. A spiritual connection is needed to bring all of these components together to access God, who is a Spirit. Without the indwelling of the Holy Spirit we cannot connect to the Spirit of God. This spiritual connection is conducted in the depths of our heart. This tabernacle of the heart is where we meet God. Some Christians create a physical place of habitation for worship. There must be a desire in the heart of the believer before we can consider to develop a physical space. This habitation is where we submit to God's authority and rest. Ephesians 2: 22 tells us, "And in you too you are being built together to become a dwelling in which God lives by his Spirit". When we build a tabernacle in our heart we are being built up and prepared for His indwelling. It is in this tabernacle that we welcome God's presence, are open to the manifestation of His power, request the Holiness of God to rest upon us, seek to be the righteousness of God, come before Him purified from the influences of the world, and most of all long in our hearts to love one another as Jesus has instructed us.

But this habitation is even more than that. Our physical bodies are a place of habitation. *Psalm 11:4* states,

"The Lord is in his Holy temple." God's place of habitation must be Holy because He is a Holy God, therefore we too must be Holy. He can not dwell in a place of corruption. *Habakkuk 2:20* states, "But the Lord is in His Holy temple; let all the earth be silent before Him". When we go into this habitation for worship, not only is the Lord there but He has also required us to be silent so that we can hear from Him. During worship we must silence ourselves to hear God's direction. The scripture in *John 2:21* reveal, "But the temple he had spoken of was His body. God dwells in those of His own." Therefore, only those who are His can sustain His habitation for worship. According to *Acts 17:24* God's word declares, "The God who made the world and everything in it, is the Lord of heaven and earth and does not live in temples built by hands." He's telling us that He does not abide in a tangible place. The author Luke wrote in *Acts 24:18*, "I was ceremonially clean when they found me in the temple courts doing this." Entering into habitation for worship requires the children of God to come unto with clean hands and pure heart. We want to be found clean for God to take up residence in us. A very familiar scripture **1 Corinthians 3:16** states, "Don't you know that you yourselves are God's temple and that God's Spirit lives in you? If anyone destroys God's temple, God will destroy him; for God's temple is sacred, and you are that temple." Believe it. God is testifying here that we are His temple, and as a result our body houses His spirit for habitation for worship. Moreover, God indicates that He will not tolerate our bodies being defiled by anything or anyone. Finally in Corinthians 6:19 God's word declares, "Do you now know that your body is a temple of the Holy Spirit, who is in you, whom you have received from God? You are not your own." This temple of habitation by God for worship was given, for His good pleasure. So whatever God does through a person during worship is subject to the Spirit which inhabits that person.

Creating a dwelling place for God requires that we surrender ourselves, specifically our thoughts and our motives. As God's dwelling place we must be emptied of all of our temporal insignificance and superficial masks. The act of emptying ourselves is not just a one-time commitment. Believers in Christ should empty them-selves not just daily, but in some instances minute by minute, and situation by situation. This process is conducted so that there are no hindrances to our worship. Hindrances to our worship circumvent the power that God has established in each of us. If we are weighted down, bound up, unavailable for God to manifest His presence, then we are not fit for the Master's use. In other words, we would not be available to be a habitation for true worship.

The children of God must recognize that when we create the "Habitation for True Worship", God will come. He will show up in all of His splendor and majesty. When we create a habitation for worship angels are revealed and we move heaven and earth. Moreover, the Glory of the Lord falls upon us in ways we cannot imagine and principalities are destroyed when we create a "Habitation for True Worship."

The creation of a habitation for God creates an atmosphere for worship. God's word declares, "that at the name of Jesus every knee should bow, in heaven and on earth and under the earth, and every tongue confess that Jesus Christ is Lord," (Philippians 2:10-11). This action comes as a result of an indwelling place for the Spirit of God to manifest Himself mightily. Our constant desire should be that we consistently be a place of habitation for "True Worship" because "thy Kingdom come, your will be done" (Matthew 6:10). Creating a habitation for worship is unlike any endeavor the children of God have ever encountered. God has ordained His original design for the habitation, the contents of the place of habitation, who the habitation is for, what is required for habitation, and what takes place in this "Habitation for True Worship." God's children don't have to do anything from a physical sense to create a "Habitation for True Worship," it is all spiritual. Every believer must get into a place to receive God's habitation and then God will create it.

Instructions from John 4:23 details to the believer that it is no longer acceptable for the believers in Christ not be a "Habitation for True Worship." Our worship services are for the habitation of God. We are not to continue to make it <u>an option</u> to invite the Lord in our worship service. Isn't He the guest of honor? Isn't He the one we come to celebrate? Welcome Him into the doors of the church and into the tabernacle of your heart so that we can experience "True Worship." God must be included in our worship service. Every child of God is required and is called to "Create a Habitation for True Worship."

X.   Jesus' worship of His Father

Some might question "what is the importance of documenting that Jesus worshipped His father"? The intent was to give an example of Jesus praying and worshipping God, or believers to partake of this experience throughout eternity. The Bible indicates in three separate, yet parallel books, of one account of Jesus worshipping His Father. These scriptures can be found in Matthew 26:36-46, Mark 14:32-42, and Luke 22: 40-46. All of these scriptures tell the story of what took place while Jesus was worshipping His father in the Garden of Gethsamane in Jerusalem.

In the description written in the Gospel of *Matthew 26:36-46,* we see several things taking place. As Jesus is about to go in to prayer and worship He tells the disciples to "stay here and keep watch with me." Our Lord and Savior Jesus Christ gave divine instruction. He's not asking the disciples as if they had a choice because they did not. Jesus is telling them to do what He requests, which is - coming into agreement. During worship, God calls all of us to come into agreement as a corporate body with the leader of the worship service. Jesus our Lord knows the seen and unseen that is about to take place. It is not that He does have the power to overcome the works of satan. He is seeking the obedience of the disciples to manifest a corporate blessing. In verse 39, "He fell with His face to the ground and prayed." This action is an act of submission in worship, from the son to the Father symbolic of Jesus' surrender to God for what was to come. In the same verse Jesus exclaims, "Yet not as I will, but as you will." Here Jesus is acknowledging God's sovereignty, accepts His position over His life, and trusts the perfect will of God. Further down in verse 41, Jesus again reminds the disciples of their purpose, to watch and pray. During worship, God does the same thing for us. God also reminds the disciples of their abilities not to fall into temptation, which can be accomplished just through daily worship.

Mark's account of what took place at Gethsamane is very similar. However, there is additional revelation concern-ing worship. In Mark 14:36 Jesus begins by saying "**Abba, Father**." These two words one of a Hebrew and one of English derivation denote Jesus' ability to submit to the Creator of all things. Jesus knows that He is the Son of God through relationship. This relationship is achieved as a result of worship. Jesus expresses to God all of His sorrow. Only when we enter into worship does the King of Kings and the Lord of Lords, our Father comfort the hearts of His children. It is here that we touch the very heart of the one who promises that we can "Cast all of our anxiety upon Him for He cares for you" (1 Peter 5:7). Verse 37 shows

Jesus chastising the disciples because during worship we are to be watchful for the manifestations of God. We are to be alert, on guard, watchmen for the manifestations of God. Saints of God we never know what will take place in worship, but we are to be alert and attentive for the move of God. During worship, we can not afford to sleep. God has promised that "indeed, He who watches over Israel will neither slumber nor sleep" (Psalm 121:4). He doesn't sleep because He is available 24 hours a day and as a result He is available seven days a week [to be worshipped.] In the latter part of verse 29, the following statement is written, "They did not know what to say to Him", because the disciples were found once again sleeping. God warns us of His obvious manifestations in worship. However, the impact of staying awake during worship is for the things that are not as obvious. In verse 41, the Apostle Mark states, "Look the Son of Man is betrayed into the hands of sinners." When Jesus worshipped His Father, God made him aware of circumstances that were not obvious to Him, and that could not be avoided. Regardless of His circumstances His first priority was to worship God.

Luke the great physicians' account of Jesus' experience at the Garden of Gethsamane was also similar to Matthew and Mark except for two points. In verse 43 the author states "An Angel from heaven appeared to Him and strengthened Him. When Jesus worshipped His Father, God released strength for the journey and also enabled Him to enter into the Holy of Holies where He could see the Heavenly Hosts that were assigned to be a messenger and protector. True Worshippers receive privileges for being obedient and seeking after God in worship. Secondly, verse 44 states, "and being in anguish, He prayed more earnestly." Jesus, Son of God, worshipped and prayed with all of His abilities during this critical moment. Regardless of His feelings, He pressed in. When we experience anguish, torment, temporary setbacks, points of affliction and even desperation, God challenges us "To press towards the mark of the most High calling, which is in Christ Jesus." Jesus pressed in with much fervor under tremendous pressure. While worshipping God, even in these circumstances, only God could give Him the strength to endure His cross. In worship, God wants us to <u>enter in</u> and give Him the burdens of our heart.

As we go boldly before His throne of grace, we are reminded in His word of the Plight of Jesus at Gethsemane. But only through worship was He able to come out victorious. Jesus, Son of God, manifested in the flesh took on the sins of the world and died for everyone. There was never, is never and will never be any exceptions to God's infinite power. But know that He is calling us to worship just as He did with His Son. This one example of Jesus worshipping His father was left to represent the relationship of Jesus with His Father and ultimate submission to God's will during worship.

Chapter 4:

"For the Father Seeketh Such to Worship Him"

Chapter 4: "For the Father Seeketh such to Worship Him"

I   Documentation of God's True Worshippers

In order to better understand what a True Worshipper is, we must first comprehend the position of their heart and their passion for worship. They have a personal relationship with God and a testimony of the impact of their worship experiences with God upon their lives. Often they testify to the love, grace, mercy, power, dominion and authority of our Lord and Savior Jesus Christ. To them worship is unconditional. Regardless of what is currently taking place in their lives they come boldly and humbly before the throne of grace to celebrate God's sovereignty in their lives. They do not perceive worship as a one-time experience in church. These Elect of God thrive upon a daily regimen of worship conducted in their secret place. True Worshippers understand that their survival is predicated upon lying at the feet of Jesus. In worship men and women come before God naked and not ashamed of who they are in Christ, or what God means to them. They are free to express their love, joy, desires, disappointments and fears. True Worshippers see God as the final judge over ever circumstance in their lives and they don't hesitate to cast all of their cares upon Him because they know He cares for Him. When a True Worshipper enters into the worship experience they are sensitized to the presence and the divine manifestation of the work being performed by God. They actively participate in the worship experience and yield them-selves to God to perform various expressions of worship through them. True Worshippers are seeking to give of themselves and not just to receive from God during worship. They understand that True Worship is the ultimate act of obedience and submission knowing, ***"But the hour cometh, and now is when the true worshippers shall worship the Father in Spirit and in truth: for the Father seeketh such to worship Him. (John 4:23)."***

In this section entitled "For the Father Seeketh such to Worship Him", the lives, experiences and passions of God's Elect True Worshippers are unveiled. True Worshippers of the Old and New Testament, as well as the 21st Century Church are examined to reveal the magnitude of their worship experiences with God. Briefly we will examine the lives of David and Anna in the Old and New Testament respectively and seven True Worshippers from God's 21st Century Church. Seven True Worshippers were asked to provide a written testimony of their personal revelation from God about worship. Included in this revelation is a personal account of their love for God, substantiation of the need of God's elect to answer the call to worship, reveal why they worship and openly disclose the relationship they have with God as a result of their worship.

From the biblical perspective worshippers were temple servants, who feared God, and yet sought to minister to Him. The account of the eleven disciples on their way to Galilee for the reading of the Great Commission in ***Matthew 28:16***, describes how when they saw Jesus they worshipped Him. A man who was spiritually blind worshipped Jesus after having a conversation with Him about his belief in the Son of man according to ***John 9:30-38***. In ***Hebrews 1:6*** the writer describes these instructions concerning God's son Jesus, "Let all God's angels worship him." And lastly, in ***Revelations 4:9-11*** John the Apostle writes the following, "Whenever the living creatures give glory, honor and thanks to him who sits on the throne and who lives for ever and ever, the twenty-four elders fall down before him who sits on the throne and worship him who lives for ever and ever." Let us now examine the lives, passion, and biblical accounts of True Worshippers.

II An Old Testament Worshipper

In the Old Testament, David a man after God's own heart was known as a True Worshipper. The story is told in *2 Samuel 6:14-15* that "David wearing a linen ephod, danced before the Lord with all his might, while he and all Israel were bringing up the ark of the Lord with shouts and the sound of trumpets." King David was in such awe of God's blessings that in *2 Samuel 6:16* it is said that he was "leaping and dancing before the Lord" as he was entering the City of David. This particular day his worship was expressed through dance, unlike his previous expression of worship which was speaking. It is said that David danced until his clothes fell off. Every bone, muscle and organ within him was used to celebrate the divine Holiness of the King of Kings and the Lord of Lords. His feet were orchestrated in a rhythmic beat that revealed the passion of this man's love for God. His body maneuvered in such a way that the people who witnessed his worship knew undeniably that he had been lead by the Spirit of God. His hands were lifted high which symbolized His surrender to the only True and Living God. David was content in knowing that He was before the God who had called, justified, glorified and sanctified him, to come into existence to worship Him. Even at the point where he was unclothed, David was secure being before God because He knew that it was in the act of worship that He was exposed to his own unrighteousness, cleansed and made whole.

III A New Testament Worshipper

The Prophetess Anna, known for her dedication, was a True Worshipper. Her faithful prayer life showed her devotion to worship. After being widowed at a young age she dedicated her life to fasting, prayer and worship in God's temple in Jerusalem according to *Luke 2:37*. While worshipping she spoke candidly about her love, appreciation and privilege to be chosen by God. She spent endless hours worshipping in the presence of God. "The customs of her time may have restricted the physical location of Anna's worship, but no earthly regulation could bind her actual worship or devotion.[16]" Her commitment to God was uncommon for her time and among women. God rewarded Anna for her obedience and commitment in worship by giving her the privileged to foretell the birth of the Messiah and to be one of the first witnesses to Jesus "just forty days after his birth, during the presentation in the temple.[17] Because of Anna's devotion to God in worship her story will last throughout eternity. This example is the work of God for a True Worshipper. Her commitment to worship prayer life far exceeded natural understanding for her time.

---

[16] Ann Spangler and Jean E. Syswerda, <u>Women of the Bible</u> (Michigan: Zondervan Publishing House, 1999) 311

[17] Ann Spangler and Jean E. Syswerda, <u>Women of the Bible</u> (Michigan: Zondervan Publishing House, 1999) 310

21st Century Worshippers' Personal Revelation

THE CALL TO WORSHIP

Evangelist. Peggy R. Carmichael, Songstress,
Gospel Music Workshop of America-
Baltimore Chapter

This **"Call to Worship"** is the reverent response of those who were in bondage and are now set free through the blood of the Lord Jesus Christ. This call from God is for His servants, for right now, because now is the time that we worship Him in Spirit and in Truth. We extol God. The worship of Him is not and will not be effective if we are not His.

Worship is not filler for a Sunday Morning Service. The Sunday Morning Service is to be *"the worship experience."* During these times where "Worship Teams" are being fully utilized to lead the congregation, it is evident that they are not effective without participants who are in relationship with God. Your relationship with God will cause you to heed to the call to Worship Him, Adore Him, Proclaim His Majesty, His Holiness and tell of His wondrous works. Your response to the call to worship will draw you to worship him for who He is! In this call, you will call the characteristics of God noteworthy to ascribe to Him the acknowledgment of His power, His position, and His excellent greatness. Free from the penalty of sin all of those that are truly his children who assume the posture of **"WORSHIP."**

*Bishop J. Charles Carrington, Jr.-Senior Pastor, Life
Builders Church and General Overseer,
Full Gospel Christian Fellowship*

I must confess, the reason that I live is to worship the Lord. He is my source, the strength of my life, my direction and my true and living God. When I was a younger man, the Lord set His hand and His purpose on me. He gave me a glimpse of His love for me as I would regularly be awakened early in the morning, around 4 a.m. with the feeling of an intense heat in the room accompanied with tremendous peace. I would know nothing but to tell Him how I felt about Him, as I would instinctively know His love towards me. This love grew into a relationship that characterizes my life as a worshipper. One could say that I am addicted to His presence, and continue our wee morning hour visits to this day.

I have found that His presence is accompanied by His complete direction. The more I worship Him, the more I am complete in His will and plan for me. While He may not reveal all at one time, He reveals Himself. That is always the one thing that I search for. In these days, it is vital that those who are Kingdom minded, completely seek His presence in worship. We not only need direction, we need power to accomplish. True power comes from the presence of the Lord. God openly reveals His presence through worship. Once one is in His presence, they become familiar with His presence. This familiarity never leads to the routine, but it makes one hungry for Him, and complete solely because of Him.

The practice of worship causes a life to be effective in the function of Kingdom assignment. We are not destined to serve ourselves, nor live as if we are the only one that matters. Our function is a part of God's plan. Our practice of worship ensures that we remain an asset to God's plan and impact this world for His glory! One should always worship. As one worships they declare who the Lord is, and How He enjoys us as well. This reciprocal relationship brings great impact upon the earth as a result of the atmosphere that is created because it is on Heaven as it is on earth.

Profile of a Worshipper
Associate Pastor Delores Golpin
Life Builders Church-Baltimore, Maryland

I was fully aware of the profile of a true worshipper as described by Jesus in John Chapter 4, but I must confess I had not initially taken it as my own. I was filled with the Holy Spirit yet feeling a void, being fed the word yet still hungry and thirsty. If this was not bad enough, I did not know at the time what the void I felt was for, nor what the hunger and thirst was for. God took me on a journey where He would teach me and show me my missing link! Through exposure to ministries where true worship (as I later came to understand it) took place, the mystery slowly began to unravel. I saw worship In Spirit and In Truth. God began to show me in my spirit what my intellect had not yet absorbed. My mind could not make sense out of what I was seeing with my eyes but my spirit immediately identified with my missing link. I began to realize what God was seeking to do in me and for me, and I began to yield my total being to Him. It was scary to give up my control and allow God to reshape my way of thinking and way of acting. God had set me free in my inner-man and taught me how to do what I was created to do, to worship the eternal God in spirit and in truth. My spirit was crying out to be free to give God everything. As I continued to submit to God, open my spirit, and follow wherever He led, I began to experience a "birthing in my spirit." I felt like something broke forth within my spirit that generated a freedom in worship that I had never known before. I discovered my true destiny and purpose in worship, my ministry, my self worth, and received my healing through worship. More importantly, through staying in the presence of God I discovered God's love for me and my love for Him, in worship.

Entering into the Secret Place
Minister Kim Y. Jackson, M. Div.

I am a True Worshipper of the Most High God committed to seeking after the heart and the face of God. When I enter into Worship I feel as though I am literally opened and exposed to receive God's power, healing and deliverance. In worship, I am free to express my love of God and to celebrate His divine nature. I am always awestruck by His presence and power. I often have an unquenchable longing to be in the presence of God to be surrounded by His comforting Spirit. I know that it is the Almighty God Himself beckoning me to come to Him. As I enter into His presence, I participate in a prelude to the manifestation of His power, through Praising and Worshipping the Most High God. He beckons me saying, "Come to me all you who are weary and burdened, and I will give you rest. Take my yoke upon you and learn from me, for I am gentle and humble in heart, and you will find rest for yours souls. For my yoke is easy and my burden is light", Matthew 11:28- 30. When I enter into the Holy of Holies behind the veil, I come into His presence celebrating him, acknowledging all of His abilities and none of my own. I expectantly "enter into His gates with thanksgiving and His courts with Praise; give thanks to Him and praise His name" Psalm 100:4." I fully acknowledge that "In your presence is fullness of joy; At your right hand are pleasures forevermore", Psalm 16:11.Through worship I rest in the assurance that "He who dwells in the secret place of the Most High Shall abide under the shadow of the Almighty", Psalm 91:1.

My Worship Experience
Pastor Steven A. Johnson, D. Min.
Abundant Faith Ministry - Baltimore, Maryland

My reason for worship is purely out of necessity. That is, it is absolutely necessary that I worship God because of who He is. My life and my reason for being is all because of Him. My purpose on this planet is to continue to find ways to express appreciation. My goal in life is not to amass a large amount of material wealth, it is to be spiritually endowed and equipped with the power to make things happen. Worship goes hand-in-hand with every-thing we do in the Body of Christ. Worship separates us from ourselves, takes us away from our problems and gives us something else to focus on…God and His goodness. Worship has to be as natural as breathing, as necessary as eating and as important as sleeping. Worship is nourishment for our Spirit. It is the regeneration of our minds. Worship is the oil for our spiritual motors; it's the spark plug that allows the body to move efficiently. Worship is an individual act of love and dedication to God. My worship is not conditional and not seasonal, but it's mandatory for my continued growth and develop-ment. Know that this may mean more to some than others, but God is looking at my heart and my intentions. I can't worship because I want something; I worship because I want to give back. This to me is more important than being a celebrity or notoriety.

Worship - by Dr. Jackie E. Miller
Prophetess and Founder of Epaphras Incorporated
Lithonia, Georgia

God created us to fellowship with Him. To worship God is to fellowship with Him. Throughout the Old Testament, worship is present as God establishes His relationship with mankind. The patriarchs built altars to worship God. God gave instructions on the place of worship. We all should have a place of personal worship outside of the church. We worship God to be close to Him, to know Him, to know His ways, to love and express our love to Him. Here is where we receive fullness of joy no matter what is going on in our lives. We enjoy His presence at the place of Worship. God enjoys being with His children. He wants to be a part of our lives. He wants to tell us things. It is sometimes difficult to envision His presence without a body to touch. Once you experience His presence, tangible presence that does not include a body, God becomes very real to you. You feel His presence all around you, no matter where you are. We are impregnated with His desires, dreams, and plans for our lives. In the place of worship, selfish ambitions disappear. He heals, delivers, and sets us free in the place of worship. We are speaking about you personal worship experience outside of the church walls. If you do not have a personal relationship with Him outside of church, worship does not occur. You cannot experience Him. At the place of worship, we receive revelation knowledge, learn the truth about matters, hear His heart, He shares His secrets, He gives us answers. He calls us friend. Are you a friend of God? God is looking for True Worshippers. (John 4:23-24)

The Model for a Worship Leader -
by Prophetess/Pastor Cassandra Montgomery, PhD.
Family Bible Ministries Worldwide, College, Institute,
Seminary, School of Counseling and University

Worship is an everyday lifestyle and you have to come into oneness with Him. Everyone cannot Worship. You have to have clean hands and a pure heart to come into worship and be open for the Spirit of God's teaching, training, edification, work of evangelism and support in Worship. To *teach* worship, the leader should teach concepts of ministering through music, music literature and music fundamentals. But the worship leader's main focus should be on teaching the word of God through the ministry of worship. Thus worship leaders must not only be worshippers and teachers of the word of God. *Training* involves help them to apply what they have been taught. The worship leader should train God's people how to worship. This includes choir rehearsal as well as for praise and worship teams. In this capacity, God's people are being trained to be song directors, conductors, and teachers, and to minister to themselves. *Edification* is the essentially building up of God's people and encouraging them. Through worship Christians are encouraged to grow in their faith, to explore ways of involvement in the various ministries of the local church and ultimately to become more like Christ. The next task for the worship leader is to proclaim the Gospel through the ministry of worship.

As a believer and a worshipper of the Lord Jesus Christ, I believe that every human being was originally created by God to worship Him and that He has given each of us a desire to love and worship. But God intended for this intimate relationship of worship to be exclusive to Him (Deuteronomy 6:4-6)., requiring a deeper understanding of who God is and who God has chosen to reveal Himself through His Son, Jesus (John 5:19, Colossians 1:15, 19). To truly worship God, believers must come to and through Jesus Christ. He is our example. Jesus, by the power of the Holy Spirit brings us into the presence of God to worship. Receiving the precious gift of salvation restores this relationship with God our Father, but to worship our Father the way He wants and deserves requires our complete and total commitment to Him.

In His encounter with the woman at the well, Jesus told the woman that she worshipped what she did not know. This means that to worship God, you must know Him and to know Him you must spend time with Him. John 4:23 confirms this point and also is the verse the Lord gave to my husband and I to begin our ministry, " But the hour is coming and now is when the true worshippers will worship the Father in spirit and in truth; for the Father is seeking such to worship Him."

True worship is desired by our Father and made available through His Son Jesus. We are required to surrender to the Holy Spirit, who will lead us into the ways of God and therefore into true worship (1Corinthians 1:10-13).

Conclusion

I do not write this document as an expert on Worship. However, through writing this book, I have come to have a deeper knowledge of what True Worship is and have come to have a deeper relationship with God. Christianity must emphasize and teach more on True Worship because it is the reason why God has created us. Christians can no longer take a passive approach to Worship and we must actively and fully participate in Worship for it is to be the lifestyle of every believer.

"The Plight of Christianity for True Worship" is real. In John 4:23, God has defined, commanded, specified a moment in time, and described the requirements for "True Worship." And yet His instructions are still not being followed. It is evident that we, the Body of Christ, still do not recognize the power and the impact of worship upon our lives. Nor do we recognize God's whole design of bringing forth the creation of man, and that is to worship Him and no other. Surely, if we had a greater comprehension of the magnitude of Worship we would find ourselves running towards the feet of Jesus at every opportunity, to worship.

Studying God's word and writing about God's command for "True Worship" has enabled me to better comprehend one of God's major biblical instructions to His people. For years I knew that I had an inherent passion for worship. I longed to be in God's presence and to celebrate His Holiness, but I couldn't fully comprehend why. Now, God has given the revelation knowledge through the Holy Spirit to understand how important it is to be obedient to His command for "True Worship." We, the Body of Christ, can no longer say we are worshipping God if we do not know what worship is, and we can no longer continue to conduct religious acts without knowing the spiritual significance. God has created us to worship Him, and that is our role in God's Kingdom.

True Worshippers *expresses their abiding love and appreciation for God and celebrate how much we value a personal and intimate relationship with Him*.

True worship is not found in music alone or in the beat of a song. It won't be found in our articulation of speech. It is found in the depths of the heart of the believer magnifying and exalting the Lord Jesus Christ. When man lays himself prostrate before God, stripped from his possessions, empty of himself, repentant, yielding to the Most High God, seeking after our Risen Lord and Savior, welcoming Him to enter into a yielded vessel, ready to be used for the master's use, then and only then are we open for True Worship and the manifestation of its purpose. Our worship should be a sweet savor to His nostrils, and a melody in His heart. Because God manifests Himself in Worship, it is here that we speak well of Him, acknowledging Him as the most High God. In worship, Christians are to be free, opening themselves up, prepared to hear from God himself. Your worship towards God should be distinguishable from everyone worshipping around you. It is personal and intimate.

Lose yourself in Worship. Worship the King of Kings and the Lord of Lords for He is Holy and Highly Exalted. Forget about yourself, the cares of the day, and worship at His feet. He is right there available any day and at any hour to worship Him. "Who may ascend into the hill of the Lord? Or who may stand in His holy place?" Psalm 24:3. So "Lift up your heads, O you gates; And be lifted up, you everlasting doors!, And the King of glory shall come in" Psalms 24:7. Come let us worship the Lord. For

He alone is worthy, for He alone is to be adored.

Oh Magnify the Lord with me. Let us exalt His Name together. God you are omnipotent and Holy. It is so easy to love you. I exalt thee. You are All Glorious, Righteous, and Pure. You are The Rock of My Salvation, Sovereign King, and Perfect in all of your ways. Lover of My Soul you are All Praise Worthy, Creator of all Creation, and Restorer of My soul. I have experienced your Healing, Strength and Might. My God you are Everything Lovely, Clothed in Majesty, How Great Thou Art.

Join the Lord's Heavenly Host in worship. Our experience with the Lord does not stop here. There is another place in God that He wants you to experience in Him, beyond our current worship. Enter into----His Secret Place----the Holy of Holies.

BIBLIOGRAPHY

Joseph Garlington, <u>Worship the Pattern of things in Heaven,</u> (Destiny Image Publishers: Pennsylvania, 2002)

Terri Law, <u>The Power of Praise and Worship</u>, (Oklahoma: Victory House, 1985)

Pastor Rod Parsley with Clint Brown, <u>Praise, the Ultimate Experience - Worship, the Ultimate Relationship</u>, (Ohio: Results Publishing, 1992) 15, 18, 55, 66, 79.

John Rea, Th.D. , <u>Charisma's Bible Handbook on the Holy Spirit</u>, Florida: Creation House, 1998) 130.

Ann Spangler and Jean E. Syswerda, <u>Women of the Bible</u> (Michigan: Zondervan Publishing House, 1999) 310-311

W.E. Vine, <u>Vine's Complete Expository Dictionary of Old and New Testament Words,</u> (Tennessee: Thomas Nelson, Inc., 1996) 234.

Vernon M. Whaley, Ph.D., <u>Understanding Music and Worship in the Local Church,</u> (Illinois: Evangelical Training Association, 2002) 5, 10, 15, 35, 61-62.

*"But the hour cometh,
and now is when the true
worshippers shall
worship the Father in
Spirit and in Truth:
for the Father seeketh
such to worship Him"
(John 4:23)*

Literary Works by Kim Y. Jackson, M. Div

In the Garden

Forty Days of Grace

True Worship – Understanding a Command
of God for a Chosen People

***Contributing Author for the Faith Anthology
Series***
Edited by Vanessa Millera

This Far by Faith

Have a Little Faith

Keeping the Faith

About the Author: *Minister Kim Y. Jackson, M. Div.* is an anointed writer, teacher, oracle and psalmist for the Lord. She has fully accepted her calling to write for the Lord, teach God's word and spread the Gospel of Jesus Christ. She stands on God's word and encourages other believers to "*Write the Vision*" (Habakkuk 2:2) that God has given to them.

As the facilitator for *Writer's Workshops* she equips attendees with the necessary tools to develop and distribute their literary works given to them by the Lord.

Attendees at her *Self-Empowerment Workshops* find balance, experience break throughs, and walk in victory as they journey through the process of healing and deliverance.

Minister Jackson has a Masters Degree in Divinity, Bachelors Degree in Christian Education, and an Associate of Arts degree in Biblical Studies from the Family Bible Ministries Worldwide, Institute, College, Seminary, School of Counseling, and University. She also has a BA degree from the University of Maryland, Baltimore County.

For more information about ordering books written by Minister Kim Y. Jackson or to book her for speaking engagements go to www.writethevizn.webs.com or email writethevizn@aol.com

Write the Vision, and make it plain on tablets,
That he may run who reads it. For the vision is yet
for an appointed time; But at the end it will speak,
and it will not lie. Though it tarries, wait for it;
Because it will surely come, It will not tarry.
Habakkuk 2:2-3(NKJV)

Made in the USA
Charleston, SC
10 December 2013